Let's Play Sports

by Janet Woodward

Harcourt
SCHOOL PUBLISHERS

Cover ©Photolibrary.com; 3 ©Alamy Images; 4 ©Getty Images; 5 ©Corbis RF;
7–8 ©Photolibrary.com; 9 ©Harcourt Schools; 10 ©Photodisc; 11 ©Harcourt Schools;
12 ©Photolibrary.com; 13 ©Harcourt Schools; 14 ©Photolibrary.com.

Printed in China

ISBN 10: 0-15-349977-X
ISBN 13: 978-0-15-349977-7

Ordering Options
ISBN 10: 0-15-349937-0 (Grade 2 ELL Collection)
ISBN 13: 978-0-15-349937-1 (Grade 2 ELL Collection)
ISBN 10: 0-15-357214-0 (package of 5)
ISBN 13: 978-0-15-357214-2 (package of 5)

4 5 6 7 8 9 10   985   15 14 13 12 11 10 09 08

Let's Play Sports

HARCOURT

Many people play sports.
Many people watch sports, too.

People like to go to games.
They cheer for their team.

People have fun playing sports. There are many different sports to play such as tennis.

Some people play team sports
like basketball or soccer.

Some people like swimming.

Some people like to walk or run in the park. Some people take their dogs with them!

You need to eat good food to play sports. A healthy diet will help you play better.

You can make lots of new friends when you play sports. Playing sports is also good exercise.

You should have fun when you
play sports.

It feels great when the ball goes high in the air, and you win the game!

Sometimes you may try really hard, but you do not win.

You should be a good sport and
not a bad loser.
Your friends and family will be
proud of you!

Scaffolded Language Development

To the Teacher

CONCEPT REVIEW Ask children what this book was mostly about. Then ask children what sports they like to play and why. Make a note on the board if they use any words from the word bank as they speak. Add any additional words from the word bank to the list and talk about the meanings of the words. Then have children use words from the word bank to complete the sentence frames below. Have them say the completed sentences chorally.

Word Bank: team, fun, friends, game, sports

1. Playing ___ keeps you fit and healthy.
2. Playing sports is a good way to make ___.
3. It is __ to play sports with friends.
4. A soccer ___ has eleven players.
5. It is great when you win the ___.

 **Social Studies**

Write a Paragraph Review with children the different reasons that people play sports. Then guide children in writing a paragraph about why sports teams are important to a community.

School-Home Connection

Talking About Sports Have children tell a family member about the book. Then suggest they talk about their favorite sport. Tell them to talk about where the sport is played, the equipment needed, and the rules.

Word Count: 154